Just Your Average Dad's Devotionals Volume 2

INSPIRING DEVOTIONALS WRITTEN BY YOUR AVERAGE DAD FOR BOTH MEN AND WOMEN

Travis Bulluck

PEACEFUL POINT MINSTRIES

Devotional Order:

I Mean Why Not?

"For I am the LORD your God who takes hold of your right hand and says to you, Do not fear; I will help you" (**Isaiah 41:13**)

We recently took a family trip to a local amusement park. As a parent, it's always fascinating to see how your children react to new rides and how brave they'll decide to be for the day. While both my son and my daughter faced a lot of fears and tried new rides, there was one interaction between my son, Bryce and sister in-law, Val that I won't forget. It was getting close to the end of the day, and Bryce had already conquered so many fears trying new things for the day. We were just getting ready to transition to the water side of the park when my sister in-law almost half jokingly looked up at the "Blast-Off" and asked Bryce if he wanted to do it.

To our entire family's surprise, Bryce immediately shot back with "I mean, sure why not". Val appeared more shocked than any of and said, "alright well let's go then." So, without batting an eye, Val and Bryce were both in line awaiting take-off!

For context, the Blast-Off is one of those rides where you get buckled into an open seat and then without much warning, you "blast off" over 185 in the air to simulate a rocket take-off. As parents, my wife and were both sitting back amused to see how things would go and to see if Bryce would chicken out at the last moment. However, like the brave little man that he is, he stayed put and even though he screamed loud enough for the entire park to hear him, he conquered the ride!

When he finished the ride, we were all very curious to get his reactions, but his face already said it all. He had the biggest smile and said it was awesome! This was an opportunity that Bryce was only able to experience because he didn't let fear get the best of him and because he knew that he had someone next to him on the ride that wasn't afraid to do it with him.

It was also an experience that got me thinking. As Christians, how many opportunities do we miss out on because we're too afraid? More importantly, why are we so afraid? I recently came across a quote that said, "F-E-A-R has two meanings: Forget Everything And Run" or Face Everything And Rise the choice is yours". Bryce chose to face his fear and literally rise. As a result, he was better for it. Unfortunately, often for most of us, when we're faced with fear we run or even worse, become paralyzed and do nothing at all. I have found that some of the reasons for allowing fear to get the best of us is because we feel like we're alone or that we're going into a situation without a guide to help us. However, the amazing news is that Isaiah 41:13 tells us that God is there for you! He wants to comfort you and hold your hand through whatever you may be afraid of today!

Whatever it is that has you afraid, turn to God! Don't let your situation cause you to run, give it to God and rise! You may just get through your situation with a smile on your face bigger than Bryce's after conquering the "Blast-Off." However, you won't know if you don't give it to God, and give it a try! When faced with something that has you afraid, give it to God, because to quote Bryce, "I mean why not?" It doesn't cost you anything other than a couple seconds of your time and it guarantees that you have someone walking side by side with you through whatever it is that has you afraid every step of the way!

Questions for Reflection:

What is one thing you're thinking about doing but are too afraid to start?

Why do we let fear hold us back?

Think about your "Blast-Off" moment. How did you feel when you conquered your fear?

In My Weakness HE is Strong

But he said to me, "My grace is sufficient for you, for my power is made perfect in weakness." Therefore I will boast all the more gladly about my weaknesses, so that Christ's power may rest on me. [10] That is why, for Christ's sake, I delight in weaknesses, in insults, in hardships, in persecutions, in difficulties. For when I am weak, then I am strong

(2 Corinthians 12: 9-10)

All throughout life we are taught that we need to be strong and not appear weak. However, in 2 Corinthians the apostle Paul is telling us the exact opposite, so what gives? Do we need to be strong all the time, or is ok to show weakness? Scratch that, not just show weakness, but boast about it. Surely Paul is crazy right? Brag about our weaknesses? At first glance, I would absolutely agree with the first assessment, which is to admit your weaknesses in fact makes you weak. However, the more that I thought about it, and reflected on my life circumstances, the more

I realized the absolute importance of admitting your weaknesses not only to others but to God. A big reason this is so important is because that if we think we're perfect, and without flaw, then we won't do anything to improve upon that.

Think about it, we've all more than likely heard the phrase "if it ain't broke don't fix it". A simple Travis translation of that is, it's working so leave it alone! Don't worry about the advancements being made all around you, this is working great!!!!! (Sarcasm) Then, the next thing you know you're being left in dust all because you failed to dig deeper into whatever it was that you were so proud of, and work to improve it. Now, instead of having to make only a few small tweaks to whatever it was that was working so well for you, you may be staring at a complete overhaul.

All because we were simply too proud to realize that while our accomplishments were awesome, there was and always is room to improve! When I wrote my first devotional and finally published it, I was beyond excited. When my first copy arrived, I couldn't even put into words how I felt. When Melanie opened it up and pointed out typos that I missed, I can't even begin to describe to you the emotions of annoyance that I felt. She began to tell me things that she noticed that I missed, and I remember saying, "Melanie not now". Then she responded with words that hit pretty deep. She said "well we need to do it if we're going to make this better".

That simple quote is exactly what acknowledging your weaknesses is all about. Acknowledging your weaknesses and areas of improvement doesn't make you weak at all; rather it brings out areas in your life that you can make better. I love what Pastor Craig Groeschel said on this topic. He said, "humility is not a sign of weakness. It is a declaration of our need for God".

Long winded Travis translation of this quote: acknowledging your weaknesses means that you're admitting you're a human and you're not perfect. It's acknowledging that you're guaranteed to screw up once or twice which is why having that relationship with God is more important than ever because God doesn't make mistakes. He absolutely wants to make you stronger in all aspects of your life. However, for him to do that, it requires a certain aspect of humility in your own life to be able to admit your flaws, every last one of them to God. It also means acknowledging that you cannot do this life on your own, nor can you overcome what you may be going through without the help of the Healer that is Jesus Christ!

By admitting your weaknesses, and improving them, either by hard work, or help from someone else you're not weak at all. You're a human being. You're flawed. You're unique. You're EXACTLY who God created you to be. By living an authentic life there is no greater witness of Christ's love, power, and strength, than admitting you in fact, may not be perfect at all.

However, we serve a mighty, mighty God who can take our weaknesses and turn them into something good. But in order for Him to do so, we need to let our guard down, and let God help us to GROW through our weaknesses so that they may in fact become our strengths! When we do that, when we admit that we are in fact weak but that HE is strong it lifts a significant burden off of our shoulders and allows us to minister to those more effectively in need. No one is perfect. Don't pretend to be!

Questions for Reflection:

What are some areas of your life that need improvement?

Why is it so hard to admit our flaws and accept constructive criticism?

How has God OR how can HE help us improve upon this?

Letting Go and Letting God

*"By faith Moses, when he had grown up, refused
to be known as the son of Pharaoh's
daughter. He chose to be mistreated along with
the people of God rather than to enjoy the
fleeting pleasures of sin. He regarded
disgrace for the sake of Christ as of greater
value than the treasures of Egypt because he
was looking ahead to his reward.* ^{27} *By faith he
left Egypt, not fearing the king's anger; he
persevered because he saw him who is
invisible. By faith he kept the Passover and the
application of blood, so that the destroyer of the
firstborn would not touch the firstborn of Israel.
By faith the people passed through the Red Sea
as on dry land; but when the Egyptians tried to
do so, they were drowned. By faith the walls of
Jericho fell, after the army had marched around
them for seven days."***(Hebrews 11:24-31)**

"You just have to keep the faith. Ohh silly child,
just have faith it will all work out." I'm sure
we've all heard those phrases at least once in our
life. The question is, what does that F word
really mean, and why do we often cringe when
someone says one of those phrases to us? Faith,

according to at least one dictionary definition is "a complete trust or confidence in someone or something". Right there, in the definition is why I believe we often cringe when someone mentions one of the above phrases. Faith-complete confidence in someone or something. The problem with that definition for most of us is that the definition of faith doesn't actually include us!

The problem is that if we try to just place faith in ourselves, we will fail. Further, when we try to put our faith in someone else, such as a politician, celebrity, or even a pastor, they. will. fail.

However, if we place our faith in God, then he will not let us down. I realize that may seem over simplified, but it really is that simple. Faith is letting go of earthly wisdom and trusting Godly wisdom! That sure sounds simple enough, and the Bible definitely provides countless examples just in the scripture shared today of individuals and situations who relied on faith in God alone to help them change or get through their circumstances. So again, I ask….. why is faith so hard?

Why is faith hard when we're faced with what seems like overwhelming odds? Why is faith so hard when we're dealing with difficult financial times? Why is faith so hard when your child or family member is acting in a way that you know they shouldn't? Why can't we just truly pray to God and TRUST that he'll take care of it? I'd like to pose to you one reason. We're humans, and we like to be in control! Faith requires us to give up control and turn it to trust, in wait for it….. GOD! Yes, I said it, we've got to give up control sometimes and let the one who created each and every one of us along with the entire world to help us.

Yupp…… I can see someone cringing right now reading this and feeling all sorts of uncomfortable realizing that there comes a point where we have to just TRUST and let God do his thing. I promise you, (even though I'll admit it's one of my absolute biggest struggles as a Christian) God will take care of what you're going through. He'll find a way to make turn your test into a testimony, your mess into a message, heck he'll find ways to make you look back and just say WOW! However, God can't do his thing, if we don't let go and give him the reigns! So please, when you hear terms like "just have faith" don't take it as a cliché phrase that people say when they don't have any other words. Take it to heart and do exactly that. Have FAITH! Give up control, and let God do his thing! He can't work if you don't give him the ability! I'll close with a song by the band Carrollton titled, "You are Faithful" that I pray serve as a powerful reminder for all of us that God is, was, and always will be faithful.

It's another day in a worn out life
With nothing lost and nothing gained
And I can't make it on my own
And that I know will never change

So my hope is in You
My trust is in You
And You have never failed

You are faithful to provide
You are always by my side

Even though I cannot see
Where You're leading me
I am Yours and You are faithful

So why do I still try my ways
When all it brings is doubt and fear?
Oh, Lord, help me see, help me believe
In You alone, I persevere

You are faithful to provide
You are always by my side
And even though I cannot see
Where You're leading me
I am Yours and You are faithful

Questions for Reflection:

Why is faith so hard?

Why is it so hard to give up control?

Think of times that you've faced struggled and God provided you a way out that you didn't see coming. Now write them down.

How do you define faith?

Join the Club

"Rejoice in the Lord always. I will say it again: Rejoice!" **(Philippians 4:4)**

"The Everything Is Great Club beats the Everything Sucks Club". That's a phrase that I heard on a podcast today. That's the phrase that absolutely gave me the gut check that I needed to get out of the pity part that I was in. It was a quote that Staff Sargent Travis Mills said on the most recent episode of my favorite podcast when he was speaking with the host, Jocko Willink discussing his life.

For context, Travis Mills was blown up while on a military operation. He lost both of his arms and his legs as a result. Mills stated that it took a while to get over it and stop being upset about it, but he eventually realized there was literally nothing he could have done differently to change what happened so what was the point of dwelling on it? He further stated that, he was particularly happy one day and then that's when the first line of this devotional came up.

Someone saw him out and Travis Mills had some extra spunk about him. This individual said something along the lines of "ohh it's Mr. everything is great over there of course you're not going to complain".   That's when Travis Mills gave his famous line. That's when hopefully that individual that was stuck in the negative changed his mind.

That story from Travis Mills made me think about what Paul said in Philippians 4:4; where for context he was writing these words while locked up in a prison! He stated not one time, but TWO times to rejoice in the Lord ALWAYS. Catch that, rejoice ALWAYS. Not sometimes, not just when it's going well, not when you hope that something good will happen, but ALWAYS. We live in an in-your-face world.

One where we constantly feel the need to share our wins on social media and one where we constantly see what others are sharing and posting on apps such as Instagram, Facebook, Pinterest, Tiktok, and Snapchat. If we're honest that can make us often lean even deeper into the everything sucks club because instead of embracing what we have and rejoicing in those things we instead wonder, why "they got lucky" and why do I not have that? Or my house would be better if it just had that. I have to ask, what good does asking those questions really do? Social media can be a powerful tool but it can also be one of the most dangerous weapons because we only see the end results. We see the filters. We see the edits.

What we don't realize is behind those filters people may also be hiding something else. We don't see that behind that success was probably a heck of a lot of failures. We don't see choices that people made where they probably missed a lot of life events to get that big promotion. Here's the key take-away for today. If you want to be happy. DON'T EVEN WORRY ABOUT WHAT SOMEONE ELSE THINKS OR DOES!

Focus on what's in your control and not on the things that you cannot control. Focus on what talents God gave you. Focus on rejoicing God daily, for the smallest of moments, through the good and the bad. Give God the praise! Rejoice.

Are you alive? Are you breathing? GOOD! That means you have another chance to get a little bit better. One more chance to make an impact on the world. One more chance to change a life! Stop living in the everything sucks club and go out and live in the Everything Is Great Club! I hear it improves your outlook quite a bit!

Questions for Reflection:

Have you found yourself caught in the "Everything Sucks Club"? What did you do to get out of it?

How much time do you spend on social media comparing your life to others?

Can it hurt to change your outlook from negative to positive?

What are three things you can do TODAY to change your outlook?

Different Gifts

6 We have different gifts, according to the grace given to each of us. If your gift is prophesying, then prophesy in accordance with your[a] faith; 7 if it is serving, then serve; if it is teaching, then teach; 8 if it is to encourage, then give encouragement; if it is giving, then give generously; if it is to lead,[b] do it diligently; if it is to show mercy, do it cheerfully.

(Romans 12:6-8)

Today's verses are some of my absolute favorites for so many reasons. One of the biggest reasons again (shocker) stems from conversations with my kiddos. Both Bryce and Peyton are incredible in their own ways and in terms of body types are built completely different. Bryce is built more like me both in his physical make-up as well as his outgoing personality. Peyton, she's just built differently, and she's got the quiet personality that her mother had for so long. Recently, Peyton just decided to stop what she was doing and start doing hand clap pushups like it was nothing. Bryce, bless his heart immediately said, "why can't I just do that".

I had to explain to him about different body types and how sometimes things come easier to other people. However, at his age, I still don't think he fully grasps it, but he still gives it everything that he's got. For Bryce it seems like for physical activities nothing comes easy to him, but he works his butt off to do his best.

However, give the boy a microphone or a group of friends to be around and he can talk your ear off! Peyton is the polar opposite. Incredibly gifted athletically but incredibly shy. The thought of being in front of people for her immediately gives her anxiety. Two children with the same parents, two totally unique and different skills to bring to the world.

Why do I share so much detail about my children here? The answer is really because when we put things in perspective of children it seems easier to understand. Of course, they're going to have different gifts and talents, they are children so we should support those talents and celebrate them! The issue becomes, as adults, rather than understand and celebrate that each person has a different gift we often times do one of the following: criticize that individual if they're better at something, put them down because of jealousy, put ourselves down because why can't we do that, or we manage to find a way to try and sabotage that person through lies, rumors, or blatant disrespect.

What Paul shares with us in Romans is so important for us to understand and embrace as believers. I would love nothing more than to be able to be an amazing singer. One that can just stop people in their tracks and demand their attention. It would definitely make my life easier and give me the ability to do pop-up church events with ease.

I, however, cannot even remotely carry a tune. So, rather than continue to force something that's not there and waste energy on a talent that I just don't have that in turn will take energy away from some of the talents that I believe God has blessed me with; I can respect and should respect that someone out there has far more talents than me in this area and reach out to them!

Let someone else use their God given gifts to bless people so that my gifts can also shine bright! You see what happens there? By acknowledging and building someone else up that may be superior to me in an area, it in turn allows them to build upon and share their own gifts while lifting a huge burden off my shoulders.

So, the challenge today is simple. Embrace the gifts that you have been blessed with. Share them with the world! If you see or know of someone that may really have a talent, let them know with some positive praise what you think so that they too can share it with the world!

The reality is, without some gentle praise from others, individuals could be missing out on using their God given gifts as they may not realize what they've been blessed with! The more we build people up, the more work we can do to advance the kingdom of God, and isn't that what we all want to be sure to do?

Questions for Reflection:

What do you believe your God given talents are?

Are you using those talents?

Why do you think God created us all with different gifts and talents?

When was the last time you gave someone a compliment?

Warning: Some Work Required

"Some time later, Jesus went up to Jerusalem for one of the Jewish festivals. ² Now there is in Jerusalem near the Sheep Gate a pool, which in Aramaic is called Bethesda[a] and which is surrounded by five covered colonnades. ³ Here a great number of disabled people used to lie—the blind, the lame, the paralyzed. [4] [b] ⁵ One who was there had been an invalid for thirty-eight years. ⁶ When Jesus saw him lying there and learned that he had been in this condition for a long time, he asked him, "Do you want to get well?"⁷ "Sir," the invalid replied, "I have no one to help me into the pool when the water is stirred. While I am trying to get in, someone else goes down ahead of me."⁸ Then Jesus said to him, "Get up! Pick up your mat and walk." ⁹ At once the man was cured; he picked up his mat and walked." **(John 5:1-8)**

Do you want to get well? Could you imagine being asked that question after someone saw you laying there in pain? Imagine going to the doctors with a massive injury, waiting for six hours to finally be seen and then having the doctor ask you, "Do you want me to make you better"? No doc, I just came here for fun! Of course I want to get better!!!!

What Jesus is asking this man who has been laying lame and invalid for years hits much deeper than just what sounds like a silly question. What Jesus is asking is a question that we should all be asking ourselves as we send out our prayers to God. Do we actually want to put in the work needed to have our prayers answered? Or are we just so accustomed to asking God for help and/or complaining about our circumstances that we'd rather just continue in that state than to believe that God can help us and actually do something about it.

Harsh, I know. But listen to how Christ talks to the invalid man. Do you want to get well? Then get up and walk! Sometimes that's the reality of faith. Do you actually believe God can help you? Then do your part in it and help yourself! God may put a door in front of you, but often times in order to get through the door you've got the put in the effort to push it open which requires not just words, but actions.

Today's devotional is really just meant to challenge you. Think about that thing that consumes you. What keeps you up at night? What holds the most time in your brain and with your conversations with God. Is it money, and getting out of debt? Is it mental health? Physical health? A relationship? We may be praying regularly to God for help and guidance, but my question today is what are YOU doing to help? For the man in this scripture, he just had to finally have the faith to get up and walk and years of misery went away BUT it took both **faith** AND **action** to see his dream of being well come true. Instead of just saying, I wish I could, I wish I could, the invalid man instead decided it was time to trust Jesus and change his circumstances. It just took a lot of faith but also a bit of work on his end too!

Questions for Reflection:

What keeps you up at night?

Why is it so easy to pray but so hard to act?

What is something actionable you can do TODAY to help push you closer to action?

Giving Right!

"Be careful not to practice your righteousness in front of others to be seen by them. If you do, you will have no reward from your Father in heaven.² "So when you give to the needy, do not announce it with trumpets, as the hypocrites do in the synagogues and on the streets, to be honored by others. Truly I tell you, they have received their reward in full. ³ But when you give to the needy, do not let your left hand know what your right hand is doing, ⁴ so that your giving may be in secret. Then your Father, who sees what is done in secret, will reward you"
(Matthew 6:1-4)

These are some of my favorite verses for several reasons. One: It talks about giving. Two: It says very simply give for the right reasons! That's the lesson today. There are so many hurting and needy people in the world. There are also so many people that have needs but are too prideful to seek out help. Sometimes, those with the most pride are those with the greatest needs, which is why it's so important that we take today's verses to heart. I truly try not to bring my children into every devotional but it's just so hard not to as they teach me so much! We were recently having family time and we talked about this exact verse with my children. Melanie explained to them in a way that only a mom can that if we give for the wrong reasons, we may be helpful in the moment, but we can actually end up doing more harm than good. Think about that for a second. The family that you helped out. It probably took everything in their power to ask you for assistance.

Do you think they'd want that information spread all over social media announcing how you just helped someone that was in dire need? Doubtful. Now, instead of coming back to you in times of trouble or feeling like they may have finally gotten the last break that they need before they're on their feet, they instead become embarrassed and go deeper into their hole of despair. Instead of turning to you or the church with victories, or in asking for private prayer requests, these individuals instead either keep it to themselves or tell the wrong crowd.

WHY? You just helped them right? WRONG. We helped ourselves. But, how Travis? I gave my hard-earned income to someone else in need I should be able to tell the world what I want. I would say, sure you absolutely can, but then did you really give it in secret, and for the right reason? I don't have the answer there, that's between you and God.

What I can say is that, when we give for the right reasons, the praise isn't important. When we give for the right reasons, we honor God. When we give for the right reasons, it can often be spontaneous and life changing! When we give WHAT God tells us to give WHEN God tells us to give there is no greater feeling of fullness in your soul. You don't need the praise of social media to know you did the right thing and feel good because God will help you feel good!

Closing this on a slightly different note, if you feel called to give, don't think about it, just do it! Often times God will place that person or thought in your mind or life at that exact moment for a very specific reason, and that one particular moment may truly be all that you have to connect and make an impact. Don't miss out because you're too busy being selfish. It's something I'm still working on every day; being more selfless and trusting that God will provide when he asks us to help! So, if you're reading this, and you NEED help, don't wait, reach out! If you're reading this and you're thinking ohh man, I should really help that person, don't wait. Do it! And don't do it for your own pleasure, do it to honor God, and he, in turn, will honor you!

Questions for Reflection:

Has there ever been a time that you just felt called to help? How did you respond?

Why do you think we feel the need to share everything we do with the world?

Have you ever been in a position of needing help?

Lessons from the Hunting Blind

"This is the day that the Lord has made; let us rejoice and be glad in it." **(Psalm 118:24)**

Do you ever have those "aha" moments where something truly clicks in your brain? For me, that often happens during hunting season. When I finally relax and let go of anything I've had going on for at least a couple hours and just enjoy looking for deer. Or having my heart jump through my chest when a squirrel plays tricks on you and gets you thinking it's a big buck running through. (Seriously, how can something so small sound so noisy?) This particular hunting season, it seemed to take me longer than it should to let go of anything that consumed my thoughts and enjoy the quite bliss of nature sitting in my stand.

Then, there was one afternoon while I was sitting in my basement, kind of miserable thinking about some tragic events that had recently occurred. I decided on a whim to ask my son (Bryce) if he wanted to go out hunting with me. He was incredibly excited and immediately said yes. So, we grabbed our gear, made sure we had warm clothes on, and made our way to the woods. When we got out there, it was hard to hide the excitement from Bryce. We got in the blind, pulled up our chairs, and just sat. We sat quietly and talked about a little bit of everything, and then, that's when Bryce called me out! I was doing what I normally do and checking my phone for any updates in the world, and he immediately yelled at me, "Dad, put your phone away! How are you going to see any deer when they come through!"

He was right! And it may sound silly, but that small little moment then led to a bigger revelation. We all get consumed with our life (and our phones) and it often in turn leads to being consumed in the wrong things that we forget to rejoice in the little things! That small reminder from Bryce led me to put my phone completely away and just talk quietly with him for the next hour without a single care in the world. What made it even better was when a deer came out in front of us. We both got super excited and watched it praying for horns. While it unfortunately turned out not to be a buck it allowed Bryce and I to have a great story to share and for Bryce to bust out in a classic 9-year-old prayer. "Dear God, please, please, please help us shoot a big buck, Amen!"

How do you not smile when you hear your son do that? While we walked out of the woods empty handed that day, we came back in with great stories to share at the dinner table, and a memory that will last us a lifetime. But, what if? What if I stayed in my sorrows and anger about the circumstances at the time? What if I stayed consumed on my phone?

What if I didn't choose to rejoice in the day that the Lord had made and instead stayed in the basement and remained miserable? I would have personally missed out on this priceless memory with my son and not been able to share his story. I wouldn't have allowed Bryce to have the same opportunity to go both back home and to school to brag about at least seeing a big deer in the woods. I would have missed an absolutely priceless moment.

I share all of this to say, life can definitely be tough and can provide its fair share of lemons. However, each day we've got a choice. We can sit alone and shut the world out, or we can go out, be thankful for the day that we have and rejoice in the Lord for another opportunity to make an impact! The choice is yours, but I can say this; fresh squeezed lemonade tastes an awfully lot better than just a plain lemon!

Questions for Reflection:

What are some ways to you can rejoice when you're feeling down?

Does technology help or hinder you feeling better?

When was the last time you rejoiced in the little things?

Identity Issues

"Yet to all who did receive him, to those who believed in his name, he gave the right to become children of God" **(John 1:12)**

I'm a runner. I enjoy every second of being on the roads or the trails with music or a podcast in my ears, pushing myself to limits both physically and mentally that I didn't know if I could surpass. However, recently I have been recovering from a nagging knee injury and haven't been able to run and it's been devasting. My wife told me that through this I would come back stronger and with more purpose and as I round out this recovery she's proven to once again be right but maybe not for the reason that she thought!

You see what I've realized as I work to recover from this setback is that I got so caught up in running that I let being a runner define who I was. I let it consume me probably more than I should. Social media posts, research, conversations, goals, EVERYTHING revolved around running. While there is absolutely nothing wrong with having goals and hobbies what is wrong is putting those goals and hobbies above God. I don't think I ever took my running obsession that far, but this time has served as a good reminder of what to prioritize and how to identify.

As Christians, our number one source of our identity is that of a child of God, which is worth rejoicing over! The entire time I've been sulking over not being able to get out and exercise I lost track of that number one and most important identity. Our hobbies, while incredibly important, don't define who we are. Our job, while a great source of income, doesn't define who we are.

What other people think, (which isn't important by the way) doesn't define who we are! Our setbacks don't define who we are! The Bible already did that for us! It told us that we are children of the one true King! And as children of God, we are fearfully and wonderfully made (Psalm 139:14).

In today's day of in-your-face social media, it's more important than ever to remember to not let things, likes, or individual reactions define

WHO you are or WHAT you become. We've already been gifted with that. We just have to accept it and set an example. In our trials and in our triumphs nothing changes. God still loves who we are. God still cares about what we do. God is and will still be with you! So, as you go about your day today, remember our identity isn't defined by things, thoughts, or others' opinions. Our identity is defined by one person, and that is our Lord Jesus Christ! Go out, rejoice, and live for him TODAY!

Questions for Reflection:

Have you ever let someone or something other than God define you?

How can your hobbies and interests turn into opportunities to show God's love?

How do you think God sees you?

Hide and Seek

*"You will seek me and find me when you seek me with all your heart" **(Jeremiah 29:13)***

A question that you may often hear from non-believers, or that you may even find yourself asking yourself sometimes is "where is God?" and truthfully, the answer is always and will always be, right in front of you! The problem that we have and why at times it seems like we can't find God is because we're not prioritizing our time seeking him. Think about one of the classic childhood games of all times, hide and seek.

The concept of the game is as the seeker you are trying to find those that may be hiding. Your primary focus is to look and find. If you find yourself distracted by outside noise, or just don't care to be playing, then chances are you're not going be able to find who you're looking for! That's exactly what this verse in Jeremiah is talking about and it serves as a great reminder to all of us. How often are we seeking God genuinely, and how often are we just "seeking" God by going through the motions? It's great to be reading your Bible and praying every day, but when you're doing that are you just doing it to check off a box, or are you doing it with an open mind and heart to let God in?

If I'm being honest, a lot of times I fall primarily into category 2. Checking the box, and in doing so, I feel good momentarily but always carry a sense of anxiety and a certain lack of peace as I go throughout my day. It's when I've got the worship music blaring, and just letting my emotions come out, that I'm genuinely seeking God, and guess what? He always shows up.

Knowing that, we need to be better as believers in ensuring that we are intentionally seeking God daily. When you pray, limit your distractions and speak from the heart. When you read, read with a purpose and ask questions. When you worship, give God all of you. The good, the bad, and the ugly. He can take it. We just must let our guard down and give it to him! We need to be intentional about seeking him and he will be there!

How is your walk with God? Do you seek him daily with all your heart, or do you let distractions of the world stop you from doing so? The challenge is a simple one today. Put away your technology or whatever distractions you have that may be limiting your ability to seek God with all your heart and then just pray. Seek out to God and do so continuously, daily, not just in the times of trouble, but in all things seek Christ. In doing so, he'll have your hand every step of the way and help you through whatever trial you're going through as well as help you triumph over the enemy! We just need to make HIM our priority!

Questions for Reflection:

What distractions are keeping you from seeking God?

What can you do to ensure that you're spending quality time with God?

How would you describe your current walk with God?

The Little Things

"It is the smallest of all seeds, but when it has grown it is larger than all the garden plants and becomes a tree, so that the birds of the air come and make nests in its branches."
(Matthew 13:32)

I was recently reminded about the verse from something that my wife whispered to me. I was having a down day for no apparent reason and she said to me, "Do you think what you do doesn't matter? I just walked upstairs and Peyton and her friend were playing with their dolls but before they could eat, both girls made sure that the dolls all bowed their heads and said a prayer".

Wow.

Something as small as making sure that each night before dinner we say a quick prayer which most of times is as simple as "Dear Lord thank for this food, help us to have a good day tomorrow, Amen" made an impact on my daughter to the point that even playing dolls they had to make sure they prayed first.

A **little** daily habit. A **HUGE** lifetime difference.

It's tough in this day and age to think that we're making an impact because we rarely see the results up front or in some cases at all. When that happens, it is easy to become discouraged, feel like what you're doing is irrelevant, just want to give up, move on, or quit all together. However, the Bible verse in Matthew makes it very clear that that even the smallest seed has to potential to grow into a tree!

As a father, I can only hope that the little things like prioritizing prayer, loving Jesus, and having family time will lead to my children accepting Christ and having the same relationship that I have with him when they grow up. I may not see those results for years to come, but both Melanie and I know that we need to continue to plant the seeds to encourage the growth.

What do you need to continue to plant the seed with? Are there things in your life that you aren't seeing an immediate impact in that have you feeling upset? Or habits that you've been working to improve but are feeling discouraged because you're not seeing the immediate impact you were hoping for?

Maybe it's becoming healthier, paying off debt, rebuilding relationships, or professional growth goals just to name a few. Don't give up. Remember a little habit done DAILY, can make a HUGE difference. We just have to remember that a seed once planted doesn't become a tree right away. It takes daily nurturing (prayer) and appropriate nutrients (Bible reading and Action) to realize its full potential. **Remember, the little things you do daily matter more than you think!**

Questions for Reflection:

What are some things that you can do to remain encouraged when the seeds you are planting don't seem to be taking root?

Are there any seeds that you previously planted that may need to be revisited?

What are some steps that you can take to not feel discouraged when you don't see the immediate results you were hoping for

Look Up

"I lift up my eyes to the mountains— where does my help come from? My help comes from the LORD, the Maker of heaven and earth."
(Psalm 121: 1-2)

I've been down lately, and I wonder who else out there can admit that? I've had so many things that I've wanted to write about but just couldn't seem to focus long enough or get my brain in the right sort of headspace to put the words to paper. However, I recently heard a sermon that gave me a not so subtle reminder as to why I've been more than likely feeling like I have.

You ready for the answer? Any guesses................

I've been spending far too much time looking down, instead of up! I know that might sound cliché but you need to understand, we all get this way. So focused on that little device in our hands that it literally pulls your head down. It serves as such a distraction from reality, and unfortunately, as a HUGE distraction from our walk with God as well. In the sermon that made me realize that getting back to writing was as simple as well, writing, Levi Lusko said the following quote. "The devil wants to keep you looking down, but the father wants you to turn to him and look up!""

I'm wondering if anyone else caught the irony in that quote? If you're feeling out of sorts, how would you describe yourself? I often, say I'm just feeling down, and when I'm feeling down then I'm just not happy and truthfully don't want to be. When I'm feeling down, I for the most part want to just remain distracted with stupid miniscule things because I think it'll help instead of working on getting to the root of what's actually bothering me. However, if you're feeling optimistic, and don't think the worlds going to come crashing down, we would often say things such as "things are looking up for me today"….. Did you catch that?

Distractions come in so many forms, and while it's absolutely okay to be busy, we need to be careful not be so busy or distracted that we've constantly got our head down and are in "go, go, go mode" because when we do, we're often missing out on doing the things that God wants us to do. More importantly, when you're feeling disconnected from God, our human response to fix that connection void seems to be that we need to become more connected than ever.... Just to the wrong things, because you know.... We're busy and can't possibly find 5 minutes to be with the Father.

Instead, we absolutely have the time to connect with other things to fill that "connection void" such as social media, too much tv, video games, scrolling aimlessly on apps, watching the news, extracurriculars, you name it, anything other than God because we just don't have the time to read a devotional, or pray, or sing worship. We're just too tired for that! (Don't laugh at the excuse because we've all been there!)

The point is simple with today's reading. **Slow down. Look up. Thank God.** I can guarantee that the maker of heaven and earth will have a few surprises in store for your life and will give you the little reminders you need that things will be alright. If you just need to turn off the outside noise, and instead look up and marvel at all of the amazing things that our God created for us! One of my absolute favorite things to do at night is to go out and just stare at the stars, even if it's only for a moment. If our God, our Creator, can create such a masterpiece as the stars in the sky, he can certainly create a masterpiece out of what you think may be the mess of your life. HOWEVER, you must understand that our HELP comes from HIM and not the things that the devil placed in our lives to distract us from turning to Jesus.

Questions for Reflection:

How much time do you spend on your phone or electronic device daily?

How much time do you spend with God daily?

What is the biggest barrier holding you back from prioritizing time with God?

Keep Moving Forward

"It pleased Darius to appoint 120 satraps to rule throughout the kingdom, ² with three administrators over them, one of whom was Daniel. The satraps were made accountable to them so that the king might not suffer loss. ³ Now Daniel so distinguished himself among the administrators and the satraps by his exceptional qualities that the king planned to set him over the whole kingdom. ⁴ At this, the administrators and the satraps tried to find grounds for charges against Daniel in his conduct of government affairs, but they were unable to do so. They could find no corruption in him, because he was trustworthy and neither corrupt nor negligent. ⁵ Finally these men said, "We will never find any basis for charges against this man Daniel unless it has something to do with the law of his God" **(Daniel 6:1-5)**

Haters gonna hate, hate, hate, hate, hate, hate….. we've all heard this song by Taylor Swift and have sung it out loud at least once or twice whether we want to admit it or not! Love it, or hate it, there are a lot of truths to these lyrics, and I think it's exactly what the Bible was speaking of in Daniel Chapter 6. I only shared one small portion of the story here, but I would encourage you to read the entire chapter.

Daniel started off as just a boy and worked his way up to one of the most trusted positions in King Darious's kingdom. More impressively, Daniel worked his way to the top by sticking to his values and continuing to honor God.

As you can imagine, Daniel's ascension towards leadership and bettering his life attracted his share of haters. So much so in fact, that this group of envious people tried to essentially trick the king into getting Daniel into trouble by knowing that he was a God honoring man. Daniel, however, remained unbothered by these attacks.

He continued to press forward with lifestyle, and most importantly, continued to put God first. Even with his enemies getting him placed into a lion's den, Daniel was undeterred. He continued with his mission, his calling, and continued his walk with the Lord and guess what the result was? The Lord literally shut the mouth of the lion and the next day when King Darius came to check on Daniel, he was shocked and excited to know that he was still alive. Moreover, king Darius issued a decree that everyone in the kingdom must fear and reverence the God of Daniel!

Dang, what a testimony! There are so many lessons that we can learn from this story. Here's the crazy thing about this world that we live in, whether we want to admit it or not there are a lot of people that want to see you fail. They'll judge you; they'll call you crazy, and even laugh if you try to do something to better yourself, your family, your career, or improve your relationship with Christ.

However, what you need to understand is that if you're truly doing something to improve your life and are putting God first then people will absolutely talk. Some for the better, some for the worse.

Why not take a page out of Daniel's playbook and give them something to talk about? Push forward with your plans. Work your butt off.

Show the world what putting God first can result in. By constantly trying to improve your life, making the world a better place, and working as hard as you can, you can unleash one powerful testimony when the time is right. That's right, that Bible verse that people put on coffee mugs is possible, because WITH GOD ALL THINGS ARE POSSIBLE!

If you're doing the right thing for the right reasons, don't worry about what other people think or say. Most of the time it's out of jealousy or fear because they know that there's something that they should be doing to improve but are too afraid or unwilling to put the work in to get the results.

Don't worry about them, instead move forward, and let your results lead to a testimony of what is possible when you leave the dreaded "comfort trap". When you put God first, people will think you're crazy, but I'd venture to say, you'd be crazy not to put God first!

Go out in the world today, set a goal, pray to God to allow that goal to honor him and be used as a testimony that you can share with others.

Then, go out and crush it! It may be scary to start, but when you understand that you've got the same God on your side that can literally shut the mouth of a lion, you'll realize even on the hardest days, when you hear the most chatter in your own brain and from those that doubt you, it's not so bad because you've got God. The hardest part is to start. So get going, and Keep. Moving. Forward!

Questions for Reflection:

How do you respond to the doubters in your life?

Is there something you're afraid to do because of what others may think or say?

What barriers prevent you from really believing that all things are possible through Christ?

But Did You Pray About It?

"But seek first his kingdom and his righteousness, and all these things will be given to you as well." **(Matthew 6:33)**

I tend to be a very impulsive person. It's something that I'm improving upon but still have a lot of work to do. How it normally works is, I get a thought in my head, it seems like a good idea or the perfect deal, and then I act on it; often thinking of the pros and cons after the action has been completed. It's not my strongest character trait, but hey, no one is perfect!

I will never forget when my impulsive nature almost got us into a new car. I was incredibly excited about it, and Melanie was on the fence. So, I did what I normally do with a big purchase. I called my parents for advice. The first words out of their mouth..... "have you prayed about it?".... I could have lied and said yes of course but I was truthful and said I had not but it was a good deal. That is when I got hit with the truth bomb that has stuck with me still to this day.... "Travis, the best thing we can say is go home, pray about it, and if it's meant to be it'll still be there for you tomorrow."

Those words are still to this day words I don't like to hear….. "It'll be there tomorrow." However, my parents were right. We did pray about it, and Mel opened up and said she didn't feel like it was the right vehicle for us so we passed on it and found something else at a better price.

It may have been a silly story but the point behind it is this; how many times do we act first and pray second? How many times do we make decisions without praying at all? Again, seeking honesty out of these devotionals, I'll admit that I'm improving but still don't "seek first his kingdom" nearly as much as I should and when I don't I find myself paying for it later on because I tried to rely on my own understanding instead of God's.

On the opposite end of the spectrum, when you pray first and act second, incredible things can happen! My wife has been feeling God poking at her to do some pretty incredible things of late. My first reaction was that she was crazy. Her response was that she continued to pray about it and the feelings that she was having were only getting stronger, so she acted, and a true blessing occurred. I honestly wonder what the outcome would have been had she of not sought God first and listened to her stupid husband instead.........

I recently saw a quote that said, "Prayer reminds us we are not in control and keeps us close to the one who is." While it certainly can be scary letting go of the steering wheel and giving it to God, that is where the growth happens. Not by our own decision making, but by having a relationship with Jesus and seeking him first. We are humans, who often seek immediate gratification and deal with the ramifications of our decisions later. God is almighty, he created us and knows our every thought. Doesn't it make more sense to get his thoughts before someone on social media? Seek God first; always, in all aspects of your life, and you may just be surprised with how things turn out! So, remember, when you are thinking about making that decision, or you have got this idea that does not go away and you are not sure what it is about, just think of my annoying little voice in your ear asking you, "But did you pray about it?" You will be thankful you did!

Questions for Reflection:

*Why do we often struggle with seeking God
when making decisions?*

*Can you name a time when you had an idea but
God had different plans after you prayed?*

*How often do you really seek God before
making a decision of any kind?*

Let's Go Wash Some Feet!

"When he had finished washing their feet, he put on his clothes and returned to his place. "Do you understand what I have done for you?" he asked them. ¹³ "You call me 'Teacher' and 'Lord,' and rightly so, for that is what I am. ¹⁴ Now that I, your Lord and Teacher, have washed your feet, you also should wash one another's feet. ¹⁵ I have set you an example that you should do as I have done for you. ¹⁶ Very truly I tell you, no servant is greater than his master, nor is a messenger greater than the one who sent him. ¹⁷ Now that you know these things, you will be blessed if you do them. "
(John 13:12-17)

Have you ever washed someone's feet before? Could you even imagine what it would be like to bend over and willingly was someone's dirty toes, especially after they were walking around barefoot or working all day? Can you imagine for a second the amount of humility it must have taken Jesus to bend over, and wash the feet of his disciples? Yes, his disciples, those same people who followed his every move. Jesus could have told these guys to give him the shirt off their backs and they would have done it BUT HE DIDN'T.

Instead, after eating a meal, and knowing that his time on this earth was coming to an end, JESUS SERVED. He didn't make the moment about him in the least. Instead, Jesus literally got on the ground and said, I am no greater than you, your feet are dirty, let me wash them!

HOLY SMOKES read that last paragraph again! I am no greater than you, so instead of being salty about my circumstances, I'm going to live a life of leadership until my last breath, proving that there is no task big or small I won't do.

I wonder, as Christians reading this, would we be humble enough to do a task that we see as below us? Maybe we'd do it, but then complain about it the entire time afterwords, right? That's not what Jesus taught here at all. When Jesus was washing the feet of his disciples it was to show them that there may be things in life that we don't like to do, and that we don't want to do, but guess what? We've got to do them, because that one event may be a powerful witness of the God we serve!

When I was younger and in youth group, our youth pastor at the time had us wash the feet of someone in the room. We had to not only clean that person's feet, but also tell them some encouraging things that we like about that person to help build them up and see their worth in God's eyes. I remember, at first, I laughed while cleaning, but then I did get serious, and had a powerful conversation with the person whose feet I was cleaning. I still do remember that moment to this day.

So, what's the point? How can you apply this to your own life? Here's what I've got for you- Sometimes it's when you're at your lowest that you can lift HIM up the highest. Sometimes, it's the smallest gestures that you do that make the greatest IMPACT. Sometimes the things that God is asking you to do may not be pretty, they may not gain you the most attention, and truthfully, there's a chance that very few people if any will even notice right away.

However, no matter how small the task, no matter what circumstance you may be in, you can absolutely be used by the kingdom of God to impact the world. You've just got to be humble enough to wash some feet and get a little dirty. You've got to make sure that you know that no task is too big or too small to be used by God. MOST IMPORTANTLY remember that no person, no matter the position of power they may be in, is too important not to serve, lead, and set the example of God's almighty love!

Questions for Reflection:

What is the first thought that comes to mind when you think about washing someone's feet?

How can you serve someone TODAY?

Have you ever felt called by God to do something but you thought it was silly? Did you go through with it? Why or Why Not?

Stay Hard When It Gets Hard

4 Then Jesus was led by the Spirit into the wilderness to be tempted[a] by the devil. After fasting forty days and forty nights, he was hungry. The tempter came to him and said, "If you are the Son of God, tell these stones to become bread. Jesus answered, "It is written: 'Man shall not live on bread alone, but on every word that comes from the mouth of God.'["Then the devil took him to the holy city and had him stand on the highest point of the temple. 6 "If you are the Son of God," he said, "throw yourself down. For it is written: 'He will command his angels concerning you, and they will lift you up in their hands, so that you will not strike your foot against a stone.'[c] "Jesus answered him, "It is also written: 'Do not put the Lord your God to the test.'[d] "Again, the devil took him to a very high mountain and showed him all the kingdoms of the world and their splendor. 9 "All this I will give you," he said, "if you will bow down and worship me."10 Jesus said to him, "Away from me, Satan! For it is written: 'Worship the Lord your God, and serve him only.'[e] "11 Then the devil left him, and angels came and attended him. (Matthew 4:1-11)

Reading today's scripture, it's safe to admit that we've all been there, right? Maybe not to the extremes that Jesus went through here, but we've had those times where you're just feeling weak, frustrated, and like nothing at all is going right. It's almost as to say you were feeling like you were under attack from the devil. Here's the thing you need to know when you feel that way. You're not alone. It's not just happening to you, and there is a way to deal with it.

We may never be as tempted by the devil as severe as Jesus was when he was alone in the wilderness. However, the fact remains that we will absolutely be tempted by the devil, and he will be sure to do it when you're already feeling low. The question becomes, how do we respond?

The answer lies on the tee-shirt my wife got me as some encouragement as I train for my first 50k race that states, "STAY HARD WHEN IT GETS HARD". What does that mean exactly? In simple terms, it means don't quit. When things get tough, you get tougher. In church terms, it means, turn to God and remember the source of peace in times of trouble. Think about it, shouldn't the answer always be to turn to God when things get tough? Absolutely. However, the shirt means all of that and then some. Too many times as a society, when things get tough, we crumble. When life gets hard instead of turning to Jesus, we walk away. When we get tired of fighting, we just quit. My question is where does that get us? What type of testimony does that provide to the world? NOWHERE.

When we're facing adversity, the challenge becomes to STAY HARD on the things that we've turned to in times of happiness and sorrow. It means when the devil comes knocking at your door, we're not running, instead we're opening up our Bibles, we're praying to God, and we're moving forward with the race that God has called us to run!

Instead of backing down, we're telling Satan, and the distractions that no weapon formed against us shall prosper! (Issaiah 54:17) and we're turning to the ONE that made us because we know that as believers we cannot get through challenges on our own. That's why it's so important that we're staying HARD to our beliefs in times of trouble because the fact is, God's word and HIS presence is the GREATEST weapon you can use against the devil. That's why the devil will continue to poke, prod, and make life miserable, because he wants you to be distracted. He wants you to let your guard down. He wants you to quit trusting the God who created you and has helped you through so many hard times.

He wants you to quit by getting you to focus on the short-term problem instead of remembering that we know the long-term solution. But why? Why would the devil care about getting us to quit so badly and to turn away from God? The answer may be beyond you. Literally. What I mean by that is, everyone can worship God when times are simple but the real testimony of your belief in the power of the God you serve is when things get difficult.

So, the devil may not care about how you respond when temptation comes, but instead, the devil is focused on limiting the impact that your testimony will have on anyone watching! (He's sneaky like that). I recently was watching a movie called "Running the Bases" and the coach said something that stuck with me. He said, "The problem with our society isn't the growing presence of evil but it's the growing absence of God's people."

You see, if Satan can eliminate the number of believers in the world through distractions and quitting, then instead of God's light prevailing, we only see the absence of light, which is darkness/evil. To change that, we've got to stop running! We must prioritize Jesus in every aspect of our life, and most importantly, we must, STAY HARD WHEN IT GETS HARD!

Questions for Reflection:

What are some things that you're running from instead of attacking head on?

Why do you think Satan focuses so much on attacking you when you're down?

How have you turned a test into a testimony?

Be Like Mary

*Mary brought in a pint of very expensive perfume made from pure nard. She poured the perfume on Jesus' feet, and then she wiped his feet with her hair. And the sweet smell from the perfume filled the whole house. **(John 12:3-6)***

I was sitting at church with my best friend, Zach and I heard the worship team sing a song called "Pour My Oil" for the very first time. When I heard it, I was instantly moved. After we left church, I still sang it. Three weeks later, it has still been on repeat. I continued to reflect on this song and to ask God (and myself) why this song has hit so deep when suddenly it started to come together.

The oil that Mary poured on Jesus wasn't some cheap knock off bottle you'd find at a local store. It was actually super expensive, and worth about a year's worth of wages. It was so costly in fact, that Judas a couple of verses later expressed his anger with Mary because he wanted to steal the perfume and sell it to make some extra money!

So, why? Why would Mary dump an entire bottle of expensive "stuff" on Jesus when she could have very simple used water? I believe it was in part because Mary knew the symbolism of the moment. She knew that Jesus' time on earth in his physical form was fleeting. She understood that the "oil" that she had, while it was definitely expensive, was just "stuff" that meant nothing compared to what Jesus was about to take on. So, Mary acted. She gave what she could, while she could, and didn't worry too much about the ramifications of no longer having "her stuff".

What a powerful example of how we should live our lives as Christians! First of all, one thing I took away from this was that Mary realized that her personal items were just fleeting, material "stuff" while what Jesus was about to do was eternal and something that you couldn't put a cost on. Let that sink in. Especially in today's day and age, where we are all chasing the next best thing. The biggest TV, the newest phone, the latest shoes, the next trend. Guess what, those things that we spend so much time chasing after and let consume us….. they'll go away. Something bigger and better will come out, you may drop it and watch it shatter and break after a short time effectively making what you were chasing useless…… then what? We end up chasing something bigger and better, ultimately falling into the trap of "it's never enough" which is a dangerous spot to be because if we're always chasing things then we're spending less time focusing on Jesus.

Mary got it.

In that moment she understood that Jesus was up to something bigger, and she felt like she needed to do something about it. Mary gave up something of materialistic value that, while may have cost a lot of money would ultimately go to waste and instead sacrificed it for the eternal value of honoring Jesus.

We need to focus on that example. In America, we want, want, want, want, and buy, buy, buy, buy but rarely do we sacrifice and actually give. Rarely do we chase after souls for Jesus, and focus on bettering our own relationships with God because we're too focused on the next new and shiny item. Those items we're chasing after, while certainly exciting and may make us feel good, can slowly become our idols if we're not careful. We save up to spend, spend too much, and then end up with nothing at all to give and a whole lot more anxiety as a result.

Be like Mary.

Give Jesus all that you have. Scripture isn't saying to not have nice things, but it is saying to make sure that we don't put those nice things above Jesus. In the moment, the perfume was all that Mary had and without hesitating she used it all to wash Jesus's feet. Would you be willing to do the same thing with your nicest item? Would you hesitate? Or would you realize everything that we have belongs to, and is because of Jesus, and make that sacrifice with a grateful heart?

I want to close today's reading with the lyrics from the song that inspired this devotional and I pray that you may just really focus on the lyrics and what they mean. Go. Be Like Mary. Give God all that you have because it's His anyways!

Take all I have, It's all
Yours anyway
I know it's not much
But God it's my everything
I pour my oil on You
I pour my oil on You

First love, You are my first
Love I don't care who's
In this room
My eyes are fixed on You

Take all I have, It's all
Yours anyway I know
It's not much, but God it's my everything I pour
My oil on You
I pour my oil on You

Doesn't matter the cost
Jesus You're worthy

Of every last drop, here is my offering I pour my
Oil on You
I pour my oil on You

Questions for Reflection:

Why is it so hard to be like Mary?

What "stuff" are you chasing after?

Do you find yourself pursuing Jesus with the same passion that you are pursuing those new items that you're wanting?

What do you need to do in order to ensure that Jesus is priority number 1?

Press On and Praise God

*This is what the Lord says: "When seventy years are completed for Babylon, I will come to you and fulfill my good promise to bring you back to this place. For I know the plans I have for you," declares the Lord, "plans to prosper you and not to harm you, plans to give you hope and a future. (**Jeremiah 29:10-11**)*

I've always loved Jeremiah 29:11. In fact, it was one of the first verses that I ever memorized and repeated outside of Joshua 1:9. The problem with taking Jeremiah 29:11 at its face though is that most people automatically read it, and think that there shouldn't be a struggle. I mean, how do you prosper and have hope if you've got to struggle at all? People love reading verse 11 but often skip over what came first in verse 10 where the Lord says AFTER 70 years! Yes..... you read that right, after 70 years of working your butt off, and struggling to get by. 70 years of hardship. THEN you will prosper!

I read that and first thought, man that must have stunk. Holding on to hope for so long while enduring so much. There had to be a point where those that were in exile thought, is it worth it? Is following God's long term plan worth this short-term suffering? As scripture rightly points out, the answer is an absolute YES, it sure is!

The question becomes though, why? Why would our loving God sit back and watch people go through hardships before promising them prosperity? Lucky for you, I've got some thoughts on this! I truly believe that God understood that if things were just given to those people that were in exile at the time, then they wouldn't truly value what they were working towards. God promises some pretty specific things in Jeremiah, and if he were just to just follow through without first seeing some growth and commitment from those seeking help, then they wouldn't have a true appreciation for God's goodness and his power.

As of this writing, I am 6 days out from completing my first ultra marathon, which will be 31 miles total. My main training is done so this week is just a low-key week where I try to recover as much as possible before tackling the big race. I am exhausted; physically, mentally, and emotionally, I am whooped from the training. However, for me, especially training for longer distance races, it's the training that molds me into the person I need to be for race day. The countless hours spent preparing, the 100's of miles ran, the injuries being managed, the money spent on making sure my body has the right nutrition, the endless conversations with Jesus on the trails, the tears spilled out in conversations with God, it's those moments that build me up and ensure that I'm ready for whatever curveballs come my way on race day. It's those moments that will help me appreciate crossing the finish line and seeing my family even more than I'll appreciate the post-race chick- fil-A after!

I honestly enjoy the training more than the race because all of that training helps me to feel prepared and also GROW so much. The training helps me know how to manage adversity when it comes my way. The training and the trials that came with it, helped give me the confidence to know that no matter what happens on race day I'm ready! The training helps me to appreciate the moment that I'm in so that when I cross the finish line, I won't take it for granted and I will shed tears. Lots of happy tears for the accomplishment!

So, does God have amazing plans in store for your life? Absolutely. The Bible clearly states it. However, when you're going through a hardship or rough season in life, don't automatically think that God has left you or abandoned you. Instead, work through the hardship that you're going through knowing that God is right by your side. When you get through whatever it is that has you down, pause, give praise to HIM, and appreciate the moment that you're in. Remember, just because you're in a trial, it doesn't mean that God isn't present which should in itself provide us with an amazing amount of hope for our future. He's always there and always will be. Let that be your hope today. Press on and Praise God!

Questions for Reflection:

Why do you think we face trials?

Have you ever had something just given to you instead of earning it? How did you feel?

Do you truly believe that even in hardships God is with you? Or have you felt at times like he wasn't present? What did God do to remind you that he was there?

Go One More

15 On the seventh day, they got up at daybreak and marched around the city seven times in the same manner, except that on that day they circled the city seven times. 16 The seventh time around, when the priests sounded the trumpet blast, Joshua commanded the army, "Shout! For the Lord has given you the city! 17 The city and all that is in it are to be devoted[b] to the Lord. (Joshua 6:15-17)

Go One More! That's the slogan of one of the running companies that I follow and it's a mantra that has really helped motivate me quite a bit. The meaning behind the saying is really quite simple. We've all got more to give so don't quit when it gets hard. Go. One. More. and then, when you're done with the next task, do another one!

Most people have probably heard the saying, "some of life's biggest blessings are on the other side of not giving up." That's not only what the phrase Go One More is about but it's also the perfect summary of Joshua walking in big circles waiting for a miracle to happen. Imagine the thoughts as the army is just walking around, not making a sound. Day after day while others are laughing at them. I'm sure they had to be thinking this is absolutely silly and thought at least more than once to attack the city or quit rather than just continue to walk. BUT THEY DIDN'T QUIT. They walked one more lap even when they were exhausted, and in doing so, the walls of Jericho crumbled, and the army took the city!

I can't help but think how this applies so much to our own lives. How many times do we miss out on what's ahead because we stop when things get uncomfortable. How many times do we then look back and wonder "what if" instead of being able to marvel at what we did through grit and God?

As I mentioned in a previous devotional, I had attempted a 50k which is approximately 31 miles. I was super pumped and felt incredibly prepared for the race but when I woke up, the weather was TERRIBLE! If I'm being honest, I felt defeated even before I started the race, but I tried it out anyway. The course was set up as 3 ten-mile loops and they were tough! The first loop I completed and felt exhausted. I started loop two and almost immediately made up my mind after starting loop two that I wouldn't be completing loop 3. I was spent both mentally, and physically. In my mind, I thought there was no possible way I could complete the race. So, after completing lap 2 I reluctantly, with tears in my eyes threw in the towel and called it a race, falling 10 miles short of my goal.

Alot of people said I should be proud of what I achieved, and I was. However, the idea of not completing something that I knew I could do if I simply kept moving forward, putting one foot in front of the other just continued to eat at me from the moment I called it quits until the moment I decided to take further action.

Two days after my incompletion of the race, I told my wife I wanted to do a "homemade 50k". I called it the Haldane Hero. 30 laps at our local park. No real fanfare (except for the crazies who showed up in the rain to cheer me on and even run a lap or two shout out to you all for the support!) Just me, God, and 6 hours and 42 minutes of moving forward in the pouring rain!

That day, I knew absolutely nothing would get in my way of achieving my goal. I knew I just had to Go. One. More. and eventually I'd get to the finish line. The moment that I finished the lap and my watch said 31 miles I felt a huge sense of accomplishment and a giant weight lifted off of my shoulders. The accomplishment felt exactly like I had hoped it would. One long, lap at a time, for 30 laps; but absolutely no quitting this time.

Life can and will be hard. When you're trying to live a life that honors God it can be even harder. There's going to be times where it just doesn't make sense and you just want to quit.

DON'T.

When things get hard, pray harder. When you want to quit, feel exhausted, or hopeless, turn your attention more to the provider of HOPE. When you feel like you just can't continue or wonder if the end results of what you're chasing after will be worth it.

GO. ONE. MORE.

I read a quote from Billy Cox that stated, "The ones who win are the ones who keep going after everyone else quits."

Exactly like what happened with Joshua's army in Jericho. They won because they didn't quit.

That's my prayer for you today. Do not quit. Continue to fight for the blessings that God promises. Put one foot in front of the other and continue to take one step at a time to achieving the promises that God has for your life. When things get tough, remember exactly why you started in the first place. For me, my why will always be to show my children what's possible when you don't give up. The most priceless moment about when I completed my race was having Bryce run 3 miles total with me and the smile on his face when we finished together. "See Dad, I told you I was going to run a 5k today."

GO. ONE. MORE.

Your outward struggles and ability to overcome them will make one heck of a testimony of what is possible with God!

Questions for Reflection:

Have you ever quit something when you knew you shouldn't have? How did you feel after?

What do you think Joshua and his army were thinking as they continued to walk circles without any action?

What is some "unfinished" business you have that you need to stick with in order to finish or take care of?

Lead…. For God's Sake

"And you yourself must be an example to them by doing good works of every kind. Let everything you do reflect the integrity and seriousness of your teaching." **(Titus 2:7)**

What is a leader, and what makes someone a good leader? Is it just a title, or is it more than that? It's been something that has been on my mind lately as I work through ensuring I'm doing the things that God wants me to be doing.

For most of my twenties and early thirties I thought that to be the leader that God called me to be, I had to be a pastor and lead a church in some capacity. There was a part of me that thought it was the only way that I could effectively reach people for Christ and make an impact on the world. I even tried my hand at it several times through various types of church plants. However, through each one of those efforts I just couldn't shake that it truly wasn't the type of "leadership" God had/has in store for my life at the moment.

Lately, I've been doing a lot of self-reflection, playing A LOT of baseball with my son, and going to A LOT of gymnastics practices with my daughter. Here's what I have come to realize; I don't have to, nor do I feel called in any way to be the leader of a church and that it's ok because my impact on God's kingdom can still be significant. Right now, for me personally in this season, my leadership role needs to focus on my family. To be present and the constant example in their lives and let God take care of the rest.

Does that role make my leadership responsibilities any less? No, I don't think so. I think it makes them that much more important in that, the way that I live MUST be the example for them because everything that I say and do is going to influence their life and decision making in a pretty significant way not only currently but in the future as well.

When thinking about leadership, I continue to go back to a quote that I heard during my time in Seminary from one of my professors, Dr. Nemitz. He said, "leadership isn't in a title it's how you lead."

Further, with this idea of effective leadership being on the forefront of my mind lately, I began re-reading the book "Lead for God's Sake" by Todd Gongwer and came across two quotes that really solidified not only what Dr. Nemitz stated, but also go along with the Bible verse in Titus. Gongwer said, "leadership in its simplest form is influence" and "if you're influencing, you're leading."

Two quotes that just hammer home the idea that no matter what we're doing, whether we want to or not, we're leading, with or without a formal title, what you do matters both when people are watching you and just as important, when no one is watching. The question is, what type of influence do you carry?

Is it the type of influence that others want to follow, or is it one in which you don't have credibility because what you say and what you do are two separate things? That's why it's so important to set an example and live a life that matches what we say we believe and value most.

The bottom line is, whether you're a coach, a pastor, a dad, a teacher, a neighbor, a son, a daughter, or you can fill in the blank with whatever you want to; you carry an influence. You don't need a title to be a leader. You don't need a formal role to do what is right or be an important figure in someone else's life. You also can never be too young or too old to lead.

We just have to lead, and that in its simplest form is to live a life that honors God by using the gifts that he has given you to influence the people that he has put in front of you. No formal title is needed for that, just simply living your life in a way that shows people the love of Jesus will make a much more significant impact on people than you think! So, don't wait for that formal title to come your way, just go, and Lead for God's sake!

Questions for Reflection:

What do you think makes a good leader?

What holds you back from leading like you know you should be?

What type of influence do you think that you carry?

Made in United States
Orlando, FL
07 October 2024

52435364R00049